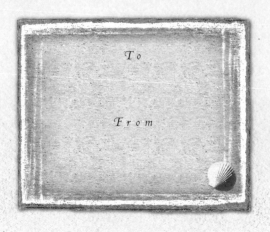

To

From

Those who hope in the LORD
    will renew their strength.
They will soar on wings like eagles;
    they will run and not grow weary,
    they will walk and not be faint.

ISAIAH 40:31

footprints

SCRIPTURE *with* REFLECTIONS

for Women

INSPIRED *by the* BEST-LOVED POEM

Ψ
inspirio™

very now and then during our devotional time my husband, Paul, and I reread the poem I wrote for him back in 1964. During these times of renewal and prayer, we talk over the events of our lives and share burdens we have for ourselves and others. Very often, we realize that the Great Shepherd has once again reached out and carried us through the day as we spend these introspective moments together.

If the pleasure of sharing these thoughts anew has taught us anything, it is this: that God's Word is true. Our Heavenly Father is faithful and will never leave us or forsake us. As we come to him daily, willing to be shaped and directed, his Word gives guideposts of clear direction. Almost everything we read, see, and experience shows us in some way that, although we do not visibly see God, he is with us. Over centuries of time others have looked back to understand that God's Spirit and presence were there, even when they felt alone.

In our quiet moments of reflection, in the fellowship of others and even in dreams, God opens the doors to our hearts. This is what happened when I originally wrote the poem, "Footprints."

After hours of wrestling with the darkness of doubt and despair, I finally surrendered to him and, in the early morning light of peace, wrote the poem as a result of that spiritual experience.

Listen for the gentle stirring of God's grace in your own mind and soul as you read these verses of encouragement. Each of us is different in our spiritual need, just as each of our days is different. God wants to place his signature on your life in a unique way. As you spend time, even just a few moments each day, reflecting on his Word, it will help you to know him better.

Spiritual growth is not so much what we have done, but the feeling of love for him we put into everything we do. It is not so much in knowing about God that we grow, but in getting to *know him* in a personal, relational way. It is in becoming "a friend of God" as Abraham did that we grow in his grace, talking with him as our companion along the way, letting God sift our thoughts and plans through the standards of his Word. May these verses encourage you anew each day as you walk with him.

Margaret Fishback Powers

footprints

One night I dreamed a dream.
I was walking along the beach with my Lord.
Across the dark sky flashed scenes from my life.
For each scene, I noticed two sets of footprints in the sand,
one belonging to me and one to my Lord.
When the last scene of my life shot before me
I looked back at the footprints in the sand
and to my surprise,
I noticed that many times along the path of my life
there was only one set of footprints.
I realized that this was at the lowest
and saddest times of my life.
This always bothered me
and I questioned the Lord about my dilemma.
"Lord, you told me when I decided to follow You,
You would walk and talk with me all the way.
But I'm aware that during the most troublesome
times of my life there is only one set of footprints.
I just don't understand why, when I needed You most,
You leave me."
He whispered, "My precious child,
I love you and will never leave you
never, ever, during your trials and testings.
When you saw only one set of footprints
it was then that I carried you."

GOD *is* WITH US...

in OUR DREAMS

❧

One night I dreamed a dream.

S ome of our dreams can have a powerful effect on us. All of us have, at one time or another, woken up laughing or fretful—and all because of a dream. The Bible tells us about many people who had dreams and visions that were given to them by God.

God said, "Listen to my words:
  When a prophet of the LORD is among you,
    I reveal myself to him in visions,
    I speak to him in dreams."

NUMBERS 12:6

[Jacob] had a dream in which he saw a stairway resting on the earth, with its top reaching to heaven, and the angels of God were ascending and descending on it. There above it stood the LORD, and he said: "I am the LORD, the God of your father Abraham and the God of Isaac. …I am with you and will watch over you wherever you go, and I will bring you back to this land. I will not leave you until I have done what I have promised you."

GENESIS 28:12–13, 15

An angel of the Lord appeared to him in a dream and said, "Joseph son of David, do not be afraid to take Mary home as your wife, because what is conceived in her is from the Holy Spirit. She will give birth to a son, and you are to give him the name Jesus, because he will save his people from their sins."

MATTHEW 1:20–21

At Gibeon the LORD appeared to Solomon during the night in a dream, and God said, "Ask for whatever you want me to give you." Solomon answered, "You have shown great kindness to your servant, my father David, because he was faithful to you and righteous and upright in heart."

1 KINGS 3:5–6

One day at about three in the afternoon Cornelius had a vision. He distinctly saw an angel of God. . . . [He later told Peter,] "Suddenly a man in shining clothes stood before me and said, 'Cornelius, God has heard your prayer and remembered your gifts to the poor. Send to Joppa for Simon who is called Peter.' . . . So I sent for you immediately, and it was good of you to come. Now we are all here in the presence of God to listen to everything the Lord has commanded you to tell us."

ACTS 10:3, 30–33

Some of our dreams are disappointing, but these are "wishful thinking" dreams, things we come up with in our own minds, circumstances or situations that we wish would happen. Only a small portion of these kinds of dreams ever come true. In fact, these dreams can be harmful if we allow them to fill us with false hope.

This is what the LORD Almighty says:
"Do not listen to what the prophets are prophesying to you;
    they fill you with false hopes.
They speak visions from their own minds,
    not from the mouth of the LORD."

JEREMIAH 23:16

We should not ignore our dreams. God will sometimes use our dreams to assure us of his promises or to tell us something about himself. And when God does speak to us in dreams, he will also help us understand them.

The word of the LORD came to Abram in a vision:
"Do not be afraid, Abram.
  I am your shield,
  your very great reward.

GENESIS 15:1

While I was still in prayer, Gabriel, the man I had
seen in the earlier vision, came to me in swift flight.
. . . He instructed me and said to me, "Daniel, I have
now come to give you insight and understanding. As
soon as you began to pray, an answer was given, which
I have come to tell you, for you are highly esteemed."

DANIEL 9:21–23

God's presence with us is a reality. Although unseen, he is with us to care for us and carry us through. As we dream our dreams with the knowledge that God is with us, we will begin to see things as Christ does and dream dreams inspired by the Holy Spirit that are worth re-telling and following. He will reassure us of his presence with us and help make those dreams come true.

GOD *is* WITH US...

in OUR DAILY WALK

❦

I was walking along the beach with my Lord.

A close walk with the Lord is an important part of a believer's life.

The LORD said, "I will walk among you and be your God, and you will be my people."

LEVITICUS 26:12

May God turn our hearts to him, to walk in all his ways and to keep the commands, decrees and regulations he gave our fathers.

1 KINGS 8:58

The LORD holds victory in store for the upright,
    he is a shield to those whose walk is blameless,
for he guards the course of the just
    and protects the way of his faithful ones.

PROVERBS 2:7–8

The Bible tells us that maintaining a close walk with God is a command we must obey, not merely a suggestion we may want to consider.

"I am God Almighty; walk before me and be blameless."

GENESIS 17:1

What does the LORD your God ask of you but to fear the LORD your God, to walk in all his ways, to love him, to serve the LORD your God with all your heart and with all your soul?

DEUTERONOMY 10:12

Walk in all the way that the LORD your God has commanded you, so that you may live and prosper and prolong your days in the land that you will possess.

DEUTERONOMY 5:33

You have declared this day that the LORD is your God and that you will walk in his ways, that you will keep his decrees, commands and laws, and that you will obey him. And the LORD has declared this day that you are his people, his treasured possession as he promised, and that you are to keep all his commands.

DEUTERONOMY 26:17–18

Be very careful to keep the commandment and the law that Moses the servant of the LORD gave you: to love the LORD your God, to walk in all his ways, to obey his commands, to hold fast to him and to serve him with all your heart and all your soul.

JOSHUA 22:5

What does the LORD require of you?
To act justly and to love mercy
   and to walk humbly with your God.

MICAH 6:8

"Obey me, and I will be your God and you will be my people. Walk in all the ways I command you, that it may go well with you."

JEREMIAH 7:23

This is love: that we walk in obedience to God's commands. As you have heard from the beginning, his command is that you walk in love.

2 JOHN 1:6

Blessed are all who fear the LORD,
   who walk in his ways.

PSALM 128:1

But what does a walk with God actually entail?
How does God want us to live?

*Love the LORD your God with all your heart and with
all your soul and with all your strength. These commandments that I give you today are to be upon your
hearts. Impress them on your children. Talk about them
when you sit at home and when you walk along the
road, when you lie down and when you get up.*

DEUTERONOMY 6:5–7

LORD, who may dwell in your sanctuary?
  Who may live on your holy hill?
He whose walk is blameless
  and who does what is righteous,
who speaks the truth from his heart
  and has no slander on his tongue,
who does his neighbor no wrong
  and casts no slur on his fellowman,
who despises a vile man
  but honors those who fear the LORD,
who keeps his oath
  even when it hurts,
who lends his money without usury
  and does not accept a bribe against the innocent.
He who does these things
  will never be shaken.

PSALM 15

Many of the things God asks us to do go against our nature. The Bible urges us to consistently walk with the Lord, walking by faith, even when it's difficult.

Just as you received Christ Jesus as Lord, continue to live in him, rooted and built up in him, strengthened in the faith as you were taught, and overflowing with thankfulness.

COLOSSIANS 2:6–7

If we walk in the light, as God is in the light, we have fellowship with one another, and the blood of Jesus, his Son, purifies us from all sin.

1 JOHN 1:7

Be strong and courageous, and do the work. Do not be afraid or discouraged, for the LORD God, my God, is with you. He will not fail you or forsake you.

1 CHRONICLES 28:20

Live a life of love, just as Christ loved us and gave himself up for us as a fragrant offering and sacrifice to God.

EPHESIANS 5:2

Jesus said, "Walk while you have the light, before darkness overtakes you. The man who walks in the dark does not know where he is going. Put your trust in the light while you have it, so that you may become sons of light."

JOHN 12:35–36

Health professionals suggest that people who want to become physically fit should try a consistent program of walking. Sustained walking several times a week will improve your muscle tone and strengthen your heart.

The Bible reassures us that our spiritual lives will also reap benefits when we are consistent in walking with the Lord.

*Live a life worthy of the L*ORD *... please him in every way: bearing fruit in every good work, growing in the knowledge of God,... and joyfully giving thanks to the Father, who has qualified you to share in the inheritance of the saints in the kingdom of light.*

COLOSSIANS 1:10–12

Jesus said, "Go and make disciples of all nations, baptizing them in the name of the Father and of the Son and of the Holy Spirit, and teaching them to obey everything I have commanded you. And surely I am with you always, to the very end of the age."

MATTHEW 28:19–20

This is what the LORD says:
"Stand at the crossroads and look;
    ask for the ancient paths,
ask where the good way is, and walk in it,
    and you will find rest for your souls."

JEREMIAH 6:16

He who walks righteously
    and speaks what is right...
this is the man who will dwell on the heights,
    whose refuge will be the mountain fortress.
His bread will be supplied,
    and water will not fail him.

ISAIAH 33:15–16

The LORD God is a sun and shield;
    the LORD bestows favor and honor;
no good thing does he withhold
    from those whose walk is blameless.

PSALM 84:11

From everlasting to everlasting
    the LORD's love is with those who fear him,
    and his righteousness with their children's
        children—
with those who keep his covenant
    and remember to obey his precepts.

PSALM 103:17–18

I command you today to love the LORD your God, to walk in his ways, and to keep his commands, decrees and laws; then you will live and increase, and the LORD your God will bless you in the land you are entering to possess.

DEUTERONOMY 30:16

Observe what the LORD your God requires: Walk in his ways ... so that you may prosper in all you do and wherever you go.

1 KINGS 2:3

I guide you in the way of wisdom
*   and lead you along straight paths.*
When you walk, your steps will not be hampered;
*   when you run, you will not stumble.*

PROVERBS 4:11–12

Blessed is the man
*   who does not walk in the counsel of the wicked*
or stand in the way of sinners
*   or sit in the seat of mockers.*
But his delight is in the law of the LORD,
*   and on his law he meditates day and night.*
He is like a tree planted by streams of water,
*   which yields its fruit in season*
and whose leaf does not wither.
*   Whatever he does prospers.*

PSALM 1:1–3

Observe the commands of the LORD your God, walking in his ways and revering him. For the LORD your God is bringing you into a good land—a land with streams and pools of water, with springs flowing in the valleys and hills; a land with wheat and barley, vines and fig trees, pomegranates, olive oil and honey; a land where bread will not be scarce and you will lack nothing.

DEUTERONOMY 8:6–9

Blessed are they whose ways are blameless,
  who walk according to the law of the LORD.
Blessed are they who keep his statutes
  and seek him with all their heart.
They do nothing wrong;
  they walk in his ways.

PSALM 119:1–3

Just as a consistent program of walking improves muscle tone and strengthens the heart, so our spiritual life will also reap benefits when we are consistent in walking with the Lord. A close walk with the Savior will ensure a sweet fellowship that will bring lasting joy, heavenly peace, and unending strength. God wants our walk with him to be joyful, shared togetherness. Such an intimate walk of faith with the Lord will assure us of his love. Our close fellowship with him will help us cross the rough places on our journey home without the slightest care.

GOD *Is* WITH US ...

DURING THE DIFFICULT TIMES

Across the dark sky flashed scenes from my life.

We all go *through* times when life seems to overwhelm us. The Bible reassures us that God's presence is with us to help us, even when we don't realize it.

The L ORD said, "My Presence will go with you, and I will give you rest."

E XODUS 33:14

In my distress I called to the L ORD,
　　and he answered me.
From the depths of the grave I called for help,
　　and you listened to my cry.

J ONAH 2:2

You are my hiding place, O L ORD;
　　you will protect me from trouble
　　and surround me with songs of deliverance.

P SALM 32:7

"Do not fear, for I am with you;
　　do not be dismayed, for I am your God.
I will strengthen you and help you;
　　I will uphold you with my righteous right hand."

I SAIAH 41:10

The LORD is my strength and my shield;
    my heart trusts in him, and I am helped.

PSALM 28:7

Moments of darkness in our lives may be caused by the death of a loved one, the loss of a job or a home or another great tragedy of life. Yet there is a greater darkness than these tragedies: the darkness in the eyes of one who has not felt God's love and grace and the assurance of his hope. There is hope for all of us. There is light. Jesus Christ, the Son of God, is our hope and light in darkness.

You are my lamp, O LORD;
    the LORD turns my darkness into light.

2 SAMUEL 22:29

The LORD will be your everlasting light,
    and your God will be your glory.

ISAIAH 60:19

You were once darkness, but now you are light in the Lord. Live as children of light.

EPHESIANS 5:8

You are a chosen people, a royal priesthood, a holy
nation, a people belonging to God, that you may declare
the praises of him who called you out of darkness into
his wonderful light.

1 PETER 2:9

The people walking in darkness
    have seen a great light;
on those living in the land of the shadow of death
    a light has dawned.

ISAIAH 9:2

In my distress I called to the LORD;
    I called out to my God.
From his temple he heard my voice;
    my cry came to his ears. . . .
He reached down from on high and took hold of me;
    he drew me out of deep waters. . . .
He brought me out into a spacious place;
    he rescued me because he delighted in me.

2 SAMUEL 22:7, 17, 20

Let him who walks in the dark,
    who has no light,
trust in the name of the LORD
    and rely on his God.

ISAIAH 50:10

Jesus said, "I have come into the world as a light, so that
no one who believes in me should stay in darkness."

JOHN 12:46

Though I have fallen, I will rise.
Though I sit in darkness,
    the LORD will be my light. ...
He will bring me out into the light;
    I will see his righteousness.

MICAH 7:8–9

Darkness covers the earth
    and thick darkness is over the peoples,
but the LORD rises upon you
    and his glory appears over you.
Nations will come to your light,
    and kings to the brightness of your dawn.

ISAIAH 60:2–3

Because of the tender mercy of our God ...
    the rising sun will come to us from heaven
to shine on those living in darkness
    and in the shadow of death,
to guide our feet into the path of peace.

LUKE 1:78–79

Our dark times may also be a time when God wants to teach us something more about ourselves and his love for us. Our faith can be strengthened if we will wait patiently and trust God's heart-desire to make us more like himself.

A righteous man may have many troubles,
but the LORD delivers him from them all.

PSALM 34:19

Our light and momentary troubles are achieving for us an eternal glory that far outweighs them all. So we fix our eyes not on what is seen, but on what is unseen. For what is seen is temporary, but what is unseen is eternal.

2 CORINTHIANS 4:17–18

We are hard pressed on every side, but not crushed; perplexed, but not in despair; persecuted, but not abandoned; struck down, but not destroyed. . . . We who are alive are always being given over to death for Jesus' sake, so that his life may be revealed in our mortal body.

2 CORINTHIANS 4:8, 11

Though you have made me see troubles,
many and bitter,
you will restore my life again;
from the depths of the earth
you will again bring me up, LORD.

PSALM 71:20

Do not be surprised at the painful trial you are suffering, as though something strange were happening to you. But rejoice that you participate in the sufferings of Christ, so that you may be overjoyed when his glory is revealed.

1 PETER 4:12–13

Be joyful in hope, patient in affliction, faithful in prayer.

ROMANS 12:12

Tragedy or testing, dark days or dreary nights, God knows what we are facing. He is in touch with what is happening to us, and he is concerned.

Though I walk in the midst of trouble,
*   you preserve my life ...*
*   with your right hand you save me, Lord*

PSALM 138:7

Jesus said, "In this world you will have trouble. But take heart! I have overcome the world."

JOHN 16:33

God's eyes are on the ways of men;
*   he sees their every step.*

JOB 34:21

God knows the way that I take;
 when he has tested me, I will come forth as gold.

JOB 23:10

I will be glad and rejoice in your love, O LORD,
 for you saw my affliction
 and knew the anguish of my soul.

PSALM 31:7

You discern my going out and my lying down;
 you are familiar with all my ways, Lord.

PSALM 139:3

The LORD will keep you from all harm—
 he will watch over your life;
the LORD will watch over your coming and going
 both now and forevermore.

PSALM 121:7–8

As we face the uncertainties that today may bring, we have the assurance that God knows what we are facing. He is in touch with what is happening to us, and he is concerned. Understand that this Heavenly Father really is caring, compassionate, comforting and concerned. Have faith in his goodness for your life and trust him with it. Be secure in the knowledge of his unconditional promises of love for you.

GOD IS WITH US ...

AS OUR CONSTANT COMPANION

*For each scene, I noticed two sets
of footprints in the sand,
one belonging to me and one to my Lord.*

I have a friend who loves to take long walks with me. We talk and laugh and enjoy each other's company as we stroll along. The exercise is beneficial, and so is the conversation.

The Lord is a lot like my friend. He enjoys walking with us as our companion on life's pathway. And he brings blessing into our lives when we walk closely with him.

The LORD is good to those whose hope is in him,
to the one who seeks him;
it is good to wait quietly
for the salvation of the LORD.

LAMENTATIONS 3:25–26

You have made known to me the path of life, Lord;
you will fill me with joy in your presence,
with eternal pleasures at your right hand.

PSALM 16:11

In my integrity you uphold me, Lord,
and set me in your presence forever.

PSALM 41:12

"You will go out with joy
and be led forth in peace;
the mountains and hills
will burst into song before you," says the LORD.

ISAIAH 55:12

Blessed are those who have learned to acclaim you,
who walk in the light of your presence, O LORD.

PSALM 89:15

Two are better than one,
because they have a good return for their work:
If one falls down,
his friend can help him up.
But pity the man who falls
and has no one to help him up!

ECCLESIASTES 4:9–10

Come ...
let us walk in the light of the LORD.

ISAIAH 2:5

The Word became flesh and made his dwelling among
us. We have seen his glory, the glory of the One and
Only, who came from the Father, full of grace and truth.

JOHN 1:14

Jesus said, "I will ask the Father, and he will give you
another Counselor to be with you forever—the Spirit
of truth. The world cannot accept him, because it nei-
ther sees him nor knows him. But you know him, for
he lives with you and will be in you."

JOHN 14:16–17

"Do not be afraid ... for I am with you and will rescue you," declares the LORD.

The awareness of God's presence with us is encouraging and heartwarming. It is as if we were two friends seated beside a rippling brook, enjoying a gentle breeze on a warm spring afternoon.

Jesus said, "Here I am! I stand at the door and knock. If anyone hears my voice and opens the door, I will come in and eat with him, and he with me."

REVELATION 3:20

Come near to God and he will come near to you.

JAMES 4:8

I am a friend to all who fear you,
*   to all who follow your precepts, Lord.*

PSALM 119:63

"Where two or three come together in my name, there am I with them," Jesus said.

MATTHEW 18:20

Jesus said, "If anyone loves me, he will obey my teaching. My Father will love him, and we will come to him and make our home with him."

JOHN 14:23

Even when we are surrounded by family and friends, some problems seem to double in size of their own accord. If we toss and turn in the early morning hours thinking about them, they become ten times as large. Yet though it seems the whole world has gone wrong around us, we are not alone—God is with us!

The eternal God is your refuge,
and underneath are the everlasting arms.

DEUTERONOMY 33:27

"As a mother comforts her child,
so will I comfort you," says the LORD.

ISAIAH 66:13

Jesus said, "I will not leave you as orphans; I will come to you."

JOHN 14:18

Cast your cares on the LORD
and he will sustain you;
he will never let the righteous fall.

PSALM 55:22

For men are not cast off
by the Lord forever.
Though he brings grief, he will show compassion,
so great is his unfailing love.
For he does not willingly bring affliction
or grief to the children of men.

LAMENTATIONS 3:31–33

I will say of the LORD, "He is my refuge and my
    fortress,
  my God, in whom *I* trust."

Be strong and courageous. Do not be terrified; do not
be discouraged, for the LORD your God will be with
you wherever you go.

JOSHUA 1:9

"Though the mountains be shaken
    and the hills be removed,
yet my unfailing love for you will not be shaken
    nor my covenant of peace be removed,"
  says the LORD, who has compassion on you.

ISAIAH 54:10

The LORD himself goes before you and will be with
you; he will never leave you nor forsake you. Do not
be afraid; do not be discouraged.

DEUTERONOMY 31:8

Jesus said, "Peace *I* leave with you; my peace *I* give
you. *I* do not give to you as the world gives. Do not
let your hearts be troubled and do not be afraid."

JOHN 14:27

"He will call upon me, and *I* will answer him;
    I will be with him in trouble,
    I will deliver him and honor him.
With long life will *I* satisfy him
    and show him my salvation," says the LORD.

PSALM 91:15–16

Where can I go from your Spirit?
    Where can I flee from your presence?
If I go up to the heavens, you are there;
    if I make my bed in the depths, you are there.
If I rise on the wings of the dawn,
    if I settle on the far side of the sea,
even there your hand will guide me,
    your right hand will hold me fast.

PSALM 139:7–10

May your unfailing love be my comfort, Lord
    according to your promise.

PSALM 119:76

Cast all your anxiety on God because he cares for you.

1 PETER 5:7

God will not let your foot slip—
    he who watches over you will not slumber. . . .
The LORD watches over you—
    the LORD is your shade at your right hand;
the sun will not harm you by day,
    nor the moon by night.
The LORD will keep you from all harm—
    he will watch over your life;
the LORD will watch over your coming and going
    both now and forevermore.

PSALM 121:3, 5–8

The L*ORD* will cover you with his feathers,
    and under his wings you will find refuge;
    his faithfulness will be your shield and rampart.

PSALM 91:4

The L*ORD* your God is with you,
    he is mighty to save.
He will take great delight in you,
    he will quiet you with his love,
    he will rejoice over you with singing.

ZEPHANIAH 3:17

The Lord enjoys walking with us as our companion on life's pathway. When we talk closely with him, his presence encourages us and warms our hearts. He is our strong provider, and he is in control of every aspect of our lives. He has promised never to leave us. He will provide for our every need. And he is stronger than any obstacle we may face, yet gentle enough to enfold us in his loving embrace. As God speaks his words of peace and blessing to our hearts, we can walk the path he has placed before us with assurance and joy.

GOD *Is* WITH US ...

THERE IS NO NEED TO LOOK BACK

When the last scene of my life shot before me I looked back at the footprints in the sand.

O nce *in a while* I find myself saying, "If only I would have …" or "Maybe I should have …" or "I wonder what would have happened if I had done …" I have to constantly remind myself that God doesn't want us to look back or regret things that happened in the past. If we live with an attitude that looks back over our lives with regrets, we are only robbing ourselves of God's mercy and assurance.

Whoever invokes a blessing in the land
    will do so by the God of truth
he who takes an oath in the land
    will swear by the God of truth.
For the past troubles will be forgotten
    and hidden from my eyes.
"Behold, I will create
    new heavens and a new earth.
The former things will not be remembered,
    nor will they come to mind," says the Lord.

ISAIAH 65:16–17

Forget the former things;
    do not dwell on the past.

ISAIAH 43:18

With God's perspective, we can trace his hand on our lives and see that he has transformed the bad things to good, just as he promised he would.

God has delivered us from such a deadly peril, and he will deliver us. On him we have set our hope that he will continue to deliver us.

2 CORINTHIANS 1:10

Jesus said, "Do not let your hearts be troubled. Trust in God; trust also in me."

JOHN 14:1

Surely God is my salvation;
    I will trust and not be afraid.
The LORD, the LORD, is my strength and my song;
    he has become my salvation.

ISAIAH 12:2

Find rest, O my soul, in God alone;
    my hope comes from him.
He alone is my rock and my salvation;
    he is my fortress, I will not be shaken.
My salvation and my honor depend on God;
    he is my mighty rock, my refuge.

PSALM 62:5–7

As we face the uncertainties that today may bring, we have the assurance that God knows what we are facing. He is in touch with what is happening to us, and he is concerned.

> *"Along unfamiliar paths I will guide them;*
> *I will turn the darkness into light before them*
> *and make the rough places smooth.*
> *These are the things I will do;*
> *I will not forsake them," says the Lord.*

ISAIAH 42:16

"I will guide him and restore comfort to him," says the LORD.

ISAIAH 57:18

A life without regrets does not mean a life without repentance. When we sin, we must go beyond regretting and feeling sorry for our actions. We must move on to repentance by turning from our sinful ways and embracing God's forgiveness.

Godly sorrow brings repentance that leads to salvation and leaves no regret.

2 CORINTHIANS 7:10

If anyone is in Christ, he is a new creation; the old has gone, the new has come!

2 CORINTHIANS 5:17

Cleanse me with hyssop, and I will be clean;
    wash me, and I will be whiter than snow. ...
Hide your face from my sins
    and blot out all my iniquity.
Create in me a pure heart, O God,
    and renew a steadfast spirit within me.
Do not cast me from your presence
    or take your Holy Spirit from me.
Restore to me the joy of your salvation
    and grant me a willing spirit, to sustain me.

PSALM 51:7, 9–12

When we have experienced God's forgiveness, we are new creatures. We do not need to live a life of regrets, but rather we can live with a forward-looking hope of glory!

Forgetting what is behind and straining toward what is ahead, I press on toward the goal to win the prize for which God has called me heavenward in Christ Jesus.

PHILIPPIANS 3:13–14

Hope does not disappoint us, because God has poured out his love into our hearts by the Holy Spirit, whom he has given us.

ROMANS 5:5

Whenever we look back over our lives, we need to do so with God's perspective rather than with an attitude of regret or "if only." We do not need to live a life of regrets. We can live with a forward-looking hope of glory! Though it may sometimes seem that things are out of control, we can always take comfort in God's enduring promises and constant presence. We can stand firm in the work of the Lord and live the life God offers us—a life free of regrets and full of joy.

Surely goodness and love will follow me
all the days of my life,
and I will dwell in the house of the LORD
forever.

PSALM 23:6

Let us draw near to God with a sincere heart in full
assurance of faith, having our hearts sprinkled to cleanse
us from a guilty conscience and having our bodies
washed with pure water. Let us hold unswervingly to the
hope we profess, for he who promised is faithful.

HEBREWS 10:22–23

GOD *Is* WITH US ...

WHEN WE FEEL ALONE

And to my surprise, I noticed that many times along the path of my life there was only one set of footprints.

T oddlers *often face* separation anxiety—a feeling of abandonment whenever their parents leave the room. Though we may be much older and wiser than little children, we still feel the pain of loneliness and isolation. Both Jesus and the psalmist also knew what it was to feel alone, abandoned and forgotten.

About the ninth hour Jesus cried out in a loud voice, "Eloi, Eloi, lama sabachthani?"—*which means,* "My God, my God, why have you forsaken me?"

MATTHEW 27:46

Jesus often withdrew to lonely places and prayed.

LUKE 5:16

Answer me quickly, O LORD.; . . .
    Do not hide your face from me. . . .
Let the morning bring me word of your unfailing love,
    for I have put my trust in you.
Show me the way I should go,
    for to you I lift up my soul.

PSALM 143:7–8

Do not hide your face from me,
    do not turn your servant away in anger;
    you have been my helper.
Do not reject me or forsake me,
    O God my Savior.

PSALM 27:9

When we feel alone and abandoned, we can take comfort in God's promises to deliver us from our isolation and pain.

He is our God
and we are the people of his pasture,
the flock under his care.

PSALM 95:7

The righteous cry out, and the LORD hears them;
he delivers them from all their troubles.

PSALM 34:17

From the LORD comes deliverance.

PSALM 3:8

I the LORD will answer them;
I, the God of Israel, will not forsake them."

ISAIAH 41:17

"Can a mother forget the baby at her breast
and have no compassion on the child she has borne?
Though she may forget,
I will not forget you!
See, I have engraved you on the palms of my hands,"
says the Lord.

ISAIAH 49:15–16

You are enthroned as the Holy One;
   you are the praise of Israel.
In you our fathers put their trust;
   they trusted and you delivered them.
They cried to you and were saved;
   in you they trusted and were not disappointed.

PSALM 22:3–5

The LORD will not reject his people, because the LORD
was pleased to make you his own.

1 SAMUEL 12:22

Keep me as the apple of your eye;
   hide me in the shadow of your wings, O LORD.

PSALM 17:8

Wait for the LORD;
   be strong and take heart
   and wait for the LORD.

PSALM 27:14

"I will be with you; I will never leave you nor forsake you," says the LORD.

JOSHUA 1:5

How great is your goodness, O LORD,
    which you have stored up for those who fear you,
which you bestow in the sight of men
    on those who take refuge in you.
In the shelter of your presence you hide them ...
    in your dwelling you keep them safe.

PSALM 31:19–20

God is always with us—in our joy and in our pain, in the good times and in the bad times. His steadfast love and faithfulness are promises we can cling to, promises to bring us joy when we face loneliness.

For this God is our God for ever and ever;
    he will be our guide even to the end.

PSALM 48:14

Consider it pure joy whenever you face trials of many kinds, because you know that the testing of your faith develops perseverance. Perseverance must finish its work so that you may be mature and complete, not lacking anything.

JAMES 1:2–4

The LORD your God is a merciful God; he will not abandon or destroy you.

DEUTERONOMY 4:31

Be strong and courageous. Do not be afraid or terrified, ... for the LORD your God goes with you; he will never leave you nor forsake you.

DEUTERONOMY 31:6

Turn to me and have mercy on me,
  as you always do to those who love your name,
    O LORD.

PSALM 119:132

The LORD is near to all who call on him,
  to all who call on him in truth.

PSALM 145:18

God is not far from each one of us. "For in him we
live and move and have our being."

ACTS 17:27–28

If ... you seek the LORD your God, you will find him
if you look for him with all your heart and with all
your soul.

DEUTERONOMY 4:29

The LORD will hear when I call to him.

PSALM 4:3

When loneliness overtakes us, we need to remember that we are not alone. God has promised to be with us. He will never forsake us. Lean on his promises and receive his peace.

I will lie down and sleep in peace,
  for you alone, O LORD,
    make me dwell in safety.

PSALM 4:8

David said about the Lord:
"I saw the Lord always before me.
  Because he is at my right hand,
  I will not be shaken."

ACTS 2:25

The LORD is with you when you are with him. If you seek him, he will be found by you.

2 CHRONICLES 15:2

Let us acknowledge the LORD;
  let us press on to acknowledge him.
As surely as the sun rises,
  he will appear;
he will come to us like the winter rains,
  like the spring rains that water the earth.

HOSEA 6:3

Do not be anxious about anything, but in everything, by prayer and petition, with thanksgiving, present your requests to God. And the peace of God, which transcends all understanding, will guard your hearts and your minds in Christ Jesus.

PHILIPPIANS 4:6–7

Grace, mercy and peace from God the Father and from Jesus Christ, the Father's Son, will be with us in truth and love.

2 JOHN 1:3

The fruit of righteousness will be peace;
  the effect of righteousness will be quietness and
  confidence forever.

ISAIAH 32:17

Why are you downcast, O my soul?
  Why so disturbed within me?
Put your hope in God,
  for I will yet praise him,
  my Savior and my God.

PSALM 42:11

The journey of life can sometimes be very troubling. We often stumble and have difficulty following in God's footsteps. Many times we feel alone in this large world. But we must never doubt God's presence with us. God will never let us down. He promises his strength, his peace and his comfort. When it seems like life is whirling out of control, we can take comfort in God's sovereignty and power. All we need to do is come to him with our seeking hearts and know that we can depend on him. We can never break God's promises by leaning on them.

GOD *Is* WITH US ...

IN OUR SORROW

I realized that this was at the lowest and saddest times of my life.

Even when things seem hopeless or impossible, God can be trusted; in Christ, he faced suffering, desolation and death. No sorrow is too deep that he cannot feel it with us and no trial is so great that he cannot deliver us from it. Though we may face trouble and difficulties, sadness and pain, God is still in control, and he is always with us.

My flesh and my heart may fail,
  but God is the strength of my heart
  and my portion forever.

PSALM 73:26

Blessed is the man who perseveres under trial, because when he has stood the test, he will receive the crown of life that God has promised to those who love him.

JAMES 1:12

When I said, "My foot is slipping,"
  your love, O LORD, supported me.
When anxiety was great within me,
  your consolation brought joy to my soul.

PSALM 94:18–19

The LORD upholds all those who fall
  and lifts up all who are bowed down.

PSALM 145:14

I sought the LORD, and he answered me;
  he delivered me from all my fears.

PSALM 34:4

We must remember to listen closely to God's voice when trouble rages around us. When the agonies of life begin to crush us, God has not moved away from us. Often we have moved away from him. We need to return to him in faith and call on him for his strength.

Return to the LORD your God,
  for he is gracious and compassionate,
slow to anger and abounding in love.

JOEL 2:13

If the LORD delights in a man's way,
  he makes his steps firm;
though he stumble, he will not fall,
  for the LORD upholds him with his hand.

PSALM 37:23–24

My soul finds rest in God alone;
  my salvation comes from him.
He alone is my rock and my salvation;
  he is my fortress, I will never be shaken.

PSALM 62:1–2

Surely, O LORD, you bless the righteous;
  You surround them with your favor
    as with a shield.

PSALM 5:12

Jesus said, "My grace is sufficient for you, for my power is made perfect in weakness."

2 CORINTHIANS 12:9

I lift up my eyes to the hills—
    where does my help come from?
My help comes from the LORD,
    the Maker of heaven and earth.

PSALM 121:1–2

Turn your ear to me, Lord,
    come quickly to my rescue;
be my rock of refuge,
    a strong fortress to save me.

PSALM 31:2

For you have been my refuge, Lord
    a strong tower against the foe.
I long to dwell in your tent forever
    and take refuge in the shelter of your wings.

PSALM 61:3–4

I will sing of your strength, O God,
    in the morning I will sing of your love;
for you are my fortress,
    my refuge in times of trouble.

PSALM 59:16

On my bed I remember you, Lord;
    I think of you through the watches of the night.
Because you are my help,
    I sing in the shadow of your wings.
My soul clings to you;
    your right hand upholds me.

PSALM 63:6–8

Look to the LORD and his strength;
    seek his face always.
Remember the wonders he has done,
    his miracles, and the judgments he pronounced.

PSALM 105:4

O LORD, be gracious to us;
    we long for you.
Be our strength every morning,
    our salvation in time of distress.

ISAIAH 33:2

The Lord stood at my side and gave me strength.

2 TIMOTHY 4:17

In the day of my trouble I will call to you,
    for you will answer me, Lord.

PSALM 86:7

Whether we face death, discouragement, loss or
pain, we can take great comfort in knowing that
no sorrow is too deep that God cannot feel it with
us. And God wants to help deliver us from it. He
wants to bring us his divine comfort.

The LORD is close to the brokenhearted
and saves those who are crushed in spirit.

PSALM 34:18

"Maidens will dance and be glad,
young men and old as well.
I will turn their mourning into gladness;
I will give them comfort and joy
instead of sorrow," says the Lord.

JEREMIAH 31:13

The LORD heals the brokenhearted
and binds up their wounds.

PSALM 147:3

Those who sow in tears
will reap with songs of joy.
He who goes out weeping,
carrying seed to sow,
will return with songs of joy,
carrying sheaves with him.

PSALM 126:5-6

Praise be to the God and Father of our Lord Jesus Christ, the Father of compassion and the God of all comfort, who comforts us in all our troubles, so that we can comfort those in any trouble with the comfort we ourselves have received from God.

2 CORINTHIANS 1:3–4

The LORD is my shepherd, I shall not be in want.
　He makes me lie down in green pastures,
he leads me beside quiet waters,
　he restores my soul.
He guides me in paths of righteousness
　for his name's sake.
Even though I walk
　through the valley of the shadow of death,
I will fear no evil,
　for you are with me;
your rod and your staff,
　they comfort me.

PSALM 23:1–4

The moon will shine like the sun, and the sunlight will be seven times brighter, like the light of seven full days, when the LORD binds up the bruises of his people and heals the wounds he inflicted.

ISAIAH 30:26

"I, even I, am he who comforts you," declares the LORD.

ISAIAH 51:12

Blessed are those who mourn,
   for they will be comforted.

MATTHEW 5:4

Jesus said, "Come to me, all you who are weary and
burdened, and I will give you rest. Take my yoke upon
you and learn from me, for I am gentle and humble
in heart, and you will find rest for your souls."

MATTHEW 11:28–29

"I will refresh the weary and satisfy the faint," says
the Lord.

JEREMIAH 31:25

The Lord will wipe every tear from their eyes. There
will be no more death or mourning or crying or pain.

REVELATION 21:4

Let the beloved of the LORD rest secure in him,
   for he shields him all day long,
     and the one the LORD loves rests between
      his shoulders.

DEUTERONOMY 33:12

Shout for joy, O heavens;
  rejoice, O earth;
  burst into song, O mountains!
For the LORD comforts his people
  and will have compassion on his afflicted ones.

ISAIAH 49:13

Jesus said, "I am the vine; you are the branches. If a man remains in me and I in him, he will bear much fruit. ... If you remain in me and my words remain in you, ask whatever you wish, and it will be given you."

JOHN 15:5, 7

The LORD gives strength to his people;
  the LORD blesses his people with peace.

PSALM 29:11

"Call upon me in the day of trouble;
  I will deliver you, and you will honor me,"
    declares the LORD.

PSALM 50:15

For I am the LORD, your God,
  who takes hold of your right hand
and says to you, Do not fear;
  I will help you.

ISAIAH 41:13

God will deliver the needy who cry out.

PSALM 72:12

The LORD helps [the righteous] and delivers them.

PSALM 37:40

The LORD has not despised or disdained
the suffering of the afflicted one;
he has not hidden his face from him
but has listened to his cry for help.

PSALM 22:24

Sorrow may cause us to doubt God's plan. Yet God reminds us that he is aware of everything that is happening to us. Whatever the circumstances, he has everything under control. And he will work his will in every circumstance. Whenever we hit rock bottom, we can rest assured of God's love and care. He hears our heartfelt cries. His encouragement can breathe new possibilities into our impossible situations. And he will answer our prayers in ways that will fill us with joy and amazement.

GOD *Is* WITH US ...

BUT SOMETIMES I WORRY.

This always bothered me ...

W hen the outlook is not good, we don't need to fret or worry. Fretting will only tie us in knots. Worry will only cast a big shadow over small problems—a shadow that should never cross our lives. We need to realize that God sees tomorrow more clearly than we see yesterday or today. The future is completely in his hands.

It is God who makes ... you stand firm in Christ. He anointed us, set his seal of ownership on us, and put his Spirit in our hearts as a deposit, guaranteeing what is to come.

2 CORINTHIANS 1:21–22

It is written:
"No eye has seen,
no ear has heard,
no mind has conceived
what God has prepared
for those who love him"—
but God has revealed it to us by his Spirit.

1 CORINTHIANS 2:9–10

"As the new heavens and the new earth that I make will endure before me," declares the LORD, "so will your name and descendants endure."

ISAIAH 66:22

"For I know the plans I have for you," declares the LORD, "plans to prosper you and not to harm you, plans to give you hope and a future."

JEREMIAH 29:11

Commit your way to the LORD;
    trust in him and he will do this:
He will make your righteousness shine like the dawn,
    the justice of your cause like the noonday sun.

PSALM 37:5–6

Commit to the LORD whatever you do,
    and your plans will succeed.

PROVERBS 16:3

Jesus said, "Do not worry about your life, what you
will eat or drink; or about your body, what you will
wear. Is not life more important than food, and the
body more important than clothes? Look at the birds of
the air; they do not sow or reap or store away in
barns, and yet your heavenly Father feeds them. Are
you not much more valuable than they?"

MATTHEW 6:25–26

Jesus said, "In the future you will see the Son of Man
sitting at the right hand of the Mighty One and
coming on the clouds of heaven."

MATTHEW 26:64

"I make known the end from the beginning,
    from ancient times, what is still to come.
I say: My purpose will stand,
    and I will do all that I please," says the Lord.

ISAIAH 46:10

Don't worry! God is with us. A new day will dawn, and the Lord will bring himself to the center of our problems.

Blessed is the man who trusts in the LORD,
whose confidence is in him.
He will be like a tree planted by the water
that sends out its roots by the stream.
It does not fear when heat comes;
its leaves are always green.
It has no worries in a year of drought
and never fails to bear fruit.

JEREMIAH 17:7–8

Dear friends, now we are children of God, and what we will be has not yet been made known. But we know that when he appears, we shall be like him, for we shall see him as he is.

1 JOHN 3:2

The plans of the LORD stand firm forever,
the purposes of his heart through all generations.

PSALM 33:11

Why, you do not even know what will happen tomorrow. What is your life? You are a mist that appears for a little while and then vanishes. Instead, you ought to say, "If it is the Lord's will, we will live and do this or that."

JAMES 4:14–15

Be still before the LORD and wait patiently for him.

PSALM 37:7

"I am concerned for you and will look on you with favor," says the LORD.

EZEKIEL 36:9

God has said,
"Never will I leave you;
* never will I forsake you."*
So we say with confidence,
"The Lord is my helper; I will not be afraid."

HEBREWS 13:5–6

Because of his great love for us, God, who is rich in mercy, made us alive with Christ.

EPHESIANS 2:4–5

Prayer is the only way to shortcut our fretting—to cut those knots of worry and care and grant us God's peace instead.

Jesus said, "Whatever you ask for in prayer, believe that you have received it, and it will be yours."

MARK 11:24

The prayer of a righteous man is powerful and effective.

JAMES 5:16

Jesus said, "Ask and it will be given to you; seek and you will find; knock and the door will be opened to you. For everyone who asks receives; he who seeks finds; and to him who knocks, the door will be opened."

MATTHEW 7:7–8

"*Call to me and I will answer you and tell you great and unsearchable things you do not know,*" says the LORD.

JEREMIAH 33:3

"*You will call upon me and come and pray to me, and I will listen to you,*" declares the LORD.

JEREMIAH 29:12

"*Before [my people] call I will answer; while they are still speaking I will hear,*" says the LORD.

ISAIAH 65:24

Jesus said, "*If you believe, you will receive whatever you ask for in prayer.*"

MATTHEW 21:22

"*They will call on my name and I will answer them; I will say, 'They are my people,' and they will say, 'The LORD is our God,'*" says the LORD.

ZECHARIAH 13:9

We must trust that the Lord will take our faith, limited as it may be, and make it into something of lasting value. We need to get our arms around God's wisdom, remember his faithfulness, and depend on his grace. Whatever our questions, whatever our circumstances, God is still in control. He will give us the answer we seek.

GOD *IS* WITH US ...

WHEN WE NEED DIRECTION

*And I questioned the Lord
about my dilemma.*

When a transit strike brought our recently purchased business to a standstill, I found myself wondering if we had made the right decision to get into this new business. The choice seemed to be the right one at the time, but now I wasn't so sure. How was I supposed to sort out what we should do next? When we face questions of this kind, we need to get our arms around God's wisdom.

If any of you lacks wisdom, he should ask God, who gives generously to all without finding fault, and it will be given to him.

JAMES 1:5

"I will instruct you and teach you in the way you should go;
I will counsel you and watch over you," says the LORD.

PSALM 32:8

Trust in the LORD with all your heart
and lean not on your own understanding;
in all your ways acknowledge him,
and he will make your paths straight.

PROVERBS 3:5–6

The LORD will guide you always;
he will satisfy your needs in a sun-scorched land
and will strengthen your frame.
You will be like a well-watered garden,
like a spring whose waters never fail.

ISAIAH 58:11

Jesus said, "When he, the Spirit of truth, comes, he will guide you into all truth. He will not speak on his own; he will speak only what he hears, and he will tell you what is yet to come."

JOHN 16:13

Show me your ways, O LORD,
    teach me your paths;
guide me in your truth and teach me,
    for you are God my Savior,
        and my hope is in you all day long.

PSALM 25:4–5

This is what the LORD says—
    your Redeemer, the Holy One of Israel:
"I am the LORD your God,
    who teaches you what is best for you,
    who directs you in the way you should go."

ISAIAH 48:17

God will teach us his ways,
    so that we may walk in his paths.

ISAIAH 2:3

Wisdom is supreme; therefore get wisdom.
    Though it cost all you have, get understanding.

PROVERBS 4:7

The LORD gives wisdom,
    and from his mouth come knowledge
        and understanding.

PROVERBS 2:6

God doesn't mind our questions when we come to him with a seeking heart. God is bigger than any question we can ask. And he often will give us the answers we seek in his Word.

Your word is a lamp to my feet
and a light for my path.

PSALM 119:105

These commands are a lamp,
this teaching is a light,
and the corrections of discipline
are the way to life.

PROVERBS 6:23

Do not let this Book of the Law depart from your mouth; meditate on it day and night, so that you may be careful to do everything written in it. Then you will be prosperous and successful.

JOSHUA 1:8

Pay attention and listen to the sayings of the wise;
apply your heart to what I teach,
for it is pleasing when you keep them in your heart
and have all of them ready on your lips.

PROVERBS 22:17–18

When we find ourselves questioning God's reason for allowing certain things to happen, we must stop, remember God's faithfulness and depend upon his grace. Whatever our questions, whatever our circumstances, God is still in control.

Know therefore that the LORD your God is God; he is the faithful God, keeping his covenant of love to a thousand generations of those who love him and keep his commands.

DEUTERONOMY 7:9

Since you are my rock and my fortress, Lord,
  for the sake of your name lead and guide me.

PSALM 31:3

Great is your love, O God, higher than the heavens;
  your faithfulness reaches to the skies.

PSALM 108:4

The LORD will fulfill his purpose for me;
  your love, O LORD, endures forever—
  do not abandon the works of your hands.

PSALM 138:8

When we need direction, we must trust that the Lord will take our faith, limited as it is, and make something of lasting value out of it. God has a plan for us. He cares about our dilemmas, hears our heartfelt cries and will answer us in ways that will astonish us and fill our hearts with songs of joy.

The LORD stilled the storm to a whisper;
  the waves of the sea were hushed.
They were glad when it grew calm,
  and he guided them to their desired haven.

PSALM 107:29–30

The job market was tight after I graduated from college, especially for an English major. I knew I wanted to use my writing and editing skills, so I tried to get into that field. But it took time. ... I was hired as an executive secretary to the software department at Zondervan Publishing House. Then I was promoted to the position of editorial assistant. ... Then a few years later I transferred to the publicity department as a writer and media coordinator. At last I was editing and writing on a daily basis! And then it was only a year and half later that a posting went up for an associate editor in the Bible department. I got the job! As I now look at this on paper, my career path appears to be systematic, logical and well planned. But truthfully, I did not have clue what was coming next. Sometimes I felt impatient and wanted to take control—do it my way. And, with each job change, the stakes seemed to get higher—I had more to lose, more to risk. Never did I imagine that, throughout the years, God was shaping me, honing my skills, preparing me. He was the one guiding my direction, each step of the way.

Catherine DeVries

GOD *Is* WITH US ...

IN OUR DECISIONS

"Lord, you told me when I decided to follow You ..."

*I*t seems that sometimes all we do is make decisions. From the time we get out of bed in the morning the day is filled with decisions. We start with deciding what we will eat for breakfast and what route we will take to get to work. Our day is usually filled with deciding what tasks take priority over others. How can God help us?

Plans fail for lack of counsel,
but with many advisers they succeed.

PROVERBS 15:22

Let the wise listen and add to their learning,
and let the discerning get guidance.

PROVERBS 1:5

Whether you turn to the right or to the left, your ears
will hear a voice behind you, saying, "This is the way;
walk in it."

ISAIAH 30:21

You guide me with your counsel, Lord,
and afterward you will take me into glory.

PSALM 73:24

Send forth your light and your truth, O God,
let them guide me;
let them bring me to your holy mountain,
to the place where you dwell.

PSALM 43:3

Where then does wisdom come from?
　Where does understanding dwell?
It is hidden from the eyes of every living thing,
　concealed even from the birds of the air. ...
God understands the way to it
　and he alone knows where it dwells.

JOB 28:20–21, 23

*I know whom I have believed, and am convinced that
the Lord is able to guard what I have entrusted to him
for that day.*

2 TIMOTHY 1:12

The decisions we need to make may be simple or
they may be complex, but they should always be
predicated on our decision to follow the Lord.

Teach me, O LORD, to follow your decrees;
　then I will keep them to the end.
Give me understanding, and I will keep your law
　and obey it with all my heart.
Direct me in the path of your commands,
　for there I find delight.

PSALM 119:33–35

Fear the LORD and serve him faithfully with all your heart; consider what great things he has done for you.

1 SAMUEL 12:24

Choose for yourselves this day whom you will serve. . . . As for me and my household, we will serve the LORD.

JOSHUA 24:15

Whatever you do, work at it with all your heart, as working for the Lord, not for men, since you know that you will receive an inheritance from the Lord as a reward. It is the Lord Christ you are serving.

COLOSSIANS 3:23–24

It is the LORD your God you must follow, and him you must revere. Keep his commands and obey him; serve him and hold fast to him.

DEUTERONOMY 13:4

A man reaps what he sows. . . . The one who sows to please the Spirit, from the Spirit will reap eternal life. Let us not become weary in doing good, for at the proper time we will reap a harvest if we do not give up. Therefore, as we have opportunity, let us do good to all people.

GALATIANS 6:7–10

When we decide to follow the Lord, it means we must live our lives the way he wants us to, following his commands, yielded to his control.

Those who live in accordance with the Spirit have their minds set on what the Spirit desires.

ROMANS 8:5

Jesus said, "As the Father has loved me, so have I loved you. Now remain in my love. If you obey my commands, you will remain in my love, just as I have obeyed my Father's commands and remain in his love. I have told you this so that my joy may be in you and that your joy may be complete."

JOHN 15:9–11

*Keep your father's commands
    and do not forsake your mother's teaching.
Bind them upon your heart forever;
    fasten them around your neck.
When you walk, they will guide you;
    when you sleep, they will watch over you;
    when you awake, they will speak to you.*

PROVERBS 6:20–22

God did not call us to be impure, but to live a holy life.

1 THESSALONIANS 4:7

Serve God with wholehearted devotion and with a willing mind, for the LORD searches every heart and understands every motive behind the thoughts.

1 CHRONICLES 28:9

The grace of God that brings salvation has appeared to all men. It teaches us to say "No" to ungodliness and worldly passions, and to live self-controlled, upright and godly lives in this present age.

TITUS 2:11–12

Just as he who called you is holy, so be holy in all you do; for it is written: "Be holy, because I am holy."

1 PETER 1:15–16

Now that you have been set free from sin, ... the benefit you reap leads to holiness, and the result is eternal life.

ROMANS 6:22

Jesus said, "Whoever has my commands and obeys them, he is the one who loves me. He who loves me will be loved by my Father, and I too will love him and show myself to him."

JOHN 14:21

Never be lacking in zeal, but keep your spiritual fervor, serving the Lord.

ROMANS 12:11

Prepare your minds for action; be self-controlled; set your hope fully on the grace to be given you when Jesus Christ is revealed.

1 PETER 1:13

Do you not know that in a race all the runners run, but only one gets the prize? Run in such a way as to get the prize. Everyone who competes in the games goes into strict training. They do it to get a crown that will not last; but we do it to get a crown that will last forever.

1 CORINTHIANS 9:24–25

Jesus said, "Be faithful, even to the point of death, and I will give you the crown of life."

REVELATION 2:10

Pursue righteousness, godliness, faith, love, endurance and gentleness. Fight the good fight of the faith.

1 TIMOTHY 6:11–12

Let us purify ourselves from everything that contaminates body and spirit, perfecting holiness out of reverence for God.

2 CORINTHIANS 7:1

Do not turn away from the LORD, but serve the LORD with all your heart.

1 SAMUEL 12:20

Let us hold unswervingly to the hope we profess, for God who promised is faithful.

HEBREWS 10:23

"*He follows my decrees
    and faithfully keeps my laws.
That man is righteous;
    he will surely live,*"
    declares the Sovereign LORD.

EZEKIEL 18:9

*Let your eyes look straight ahead,
    fix your gaze directly before you.
Make level paths for your feet
    and take only ways that are firm.*

PROVERBS 4:25–26

"*I will give you a new heart and put a new spirit in
you; I will remove from you your heart of stone and
give you a heart of flesh. And I will put my Spirit in
you and move you to follow my decrees and be careful to keep my laws,*" *declares the Lord.*

EZEKIEL 36:26–27

*LORD, who may dwell in your sanctuary?
    Who may live on your holy hill?
He whose walk is blameless
    and who does what is righteous,
who speaks the truth from his heart.*

PSALM 15:1–2

Now all has been heard;
    here is the conclusion of the matter:
Fear God and keep his commandments,
    for this is the whole duty of man.

ECCLESIASTES 12:13

The fruit of the Spirit is love, joy, peace, patience, kindness, goodness, faithfulness, gentleness and self-control. ... Since we live by the Spirit, let us keep in step with the Spirit.

GALATIANS 5:22–23, 25

If anyone obeys his word, God's love is truly made complete in him.

1 JOHN 2:5

Let the word of Christ dwell in you richly as you teach and admonish one another with all wisdom, and as you sing psalms, hymns and spiritual songs with gratitude in your hearts to God. And whatever you do, whether in word or deed, do it all in the name of the Lord Jesus, giving thanks to God the Father through him.

COLOSSIANS 3:16–17

Jesus said, "Blessed ... are those who hear the word of God and obey it."

LUKE 11:28

We all need God's divine power from day to day to
follow in his footsteps ... so that we may make
decisions based on his character and ultimately
share in his glory.

*If anyone speaks, he should do it as one speaking the
very words of God. If anyone serves, he should do it
with the strength God provides, so that in all things
God may be praised through Jesus Christ.*

1 PETER 4:11

Decisions, decisions, decisions. It sometimes seems
that all we do is make decisions. Some decisions
may be simple; others may be complex. Yet sometimes the right choice may be obscure. We need
someone to help tell us what to do. When we face
decisions of all kinds, we should make sure to pred-
icate our choices on our decision to follow the
Lord. He will show us how to follow in his steps.
Following the Lord, means living your life the way
he wants you to, yielding to his control in every situation. When we consistently walk with the Lord,
we will find clear direction, joyful hearts, and the
assurance of God's presence in every circumstance.

GOD *Is* WITH US ...

TO PROVIDE GUIDANCE

"... You would walk and talk with me all the way."

I saw two *children walking* together today, happily exchanging words and glances, laughing aloud at shared jokes. They didn't worry about the cracks in the sidewalk or the bumps in the road, but rather skipped along over them. God wants our walk with him to be just like that—enjoying his company, sharing together and crossing the rough places on our journey home without the slightest care.

God guides the humble in what is right
and teaches them his way.

PSALM 25:9

Righteousness goes before the LORD
and prepares the way for his steps.

PSALM 85:13

Remember, O LORD, how I have walked before you faithfully and with wholehearted devotion and have done what is good in your eyes.

2 KINGS 20:3

Because of your great compassion you did not aban-don [your people] in the desert. By day the pillar of cloud did not cease to guide them on their path, nor the pillar of fire by night to shine on the way they were to take. You gave your good Spirit to instruct them.

NEHEMIAH 9:19—20

Teach me your way, O LORD;
  lead me in a straight path.

PSALM 27:11

Teach me to do your will,
  for you are my God;
may your good Spirit
  lead me on level ground.

PSALM 143:10

You have delivered me from death
  and my feet from stumbling,
that I may walk before God
  in the light of life.

PSALM 56:13

May the nations be glad and sing for joy,
  for you rule the peoples justly, Lord,
  and guide the nations of the earth.

PSALM 67:4

Sometimes we need someone to help show us the way. That someone is God.

In your unfailing love you will lead
  the people you have redeemed, O LORD.
In your strength your will guide them
  to your holy dwelling.

EXODUS 15:13

Lead me, O LORD, in your righteousness . . .
   make straight your way before me.

PSALM 5:8

God who has compassion on [his people] will guide them
   and lead them beside springs of water.

ISAIAH 49:10

By day the Lord went ahead of them in a pillar of cloud
to guide them on their way and by night in a pillar of
fire to give them light, so that they could travel by day or
night. Neither the pillar of cloud by day nor the pillar
of fire by night left its place in front of the people.

EXODUS 13:21–22

You have made known to me the paths of life;
   you will fill me with joy in your presence, Lord.

ACTS 2:28

God guided them safely, so they were unafraid.

PSALM 78:53

Thanks be to God, who always leads us in triumphal
procession in Christ and through us spreads everywhere
the fragrance of the knowledge of him.

2 CORINTHIANS 2:14

"I will give you shepherds after my own heart, who
will lead you with knowledge and understanding," says
the LORD.

JEREMIAH 3:15

The path of the righteous is like the first gleam
    of dawn,
    shining ever brighter till the full light of day.

PROVERBS 4:18

"I will lead them beside streams of water
    on a level path where they will not stumble,"
    says the Lord.

JEREMIAH 31:9

Those who are wise will shine like the brightness of
the heavens, and those who lead many to righteousness,
like the stars for ever and ever.

DANIEL 12:3

May the Lord direct your hearts into God's love and
Christ's perseverance.

2 THESSALONIANS 3:5

I know, O LORD, that a man's life is not his own;
    it is not for man to direct his steps.

JEREMIAH 10:23

Direct my footsteps according to your word, O LORD.

PSALM 119:133

A man's steps are directed by the LORD.

PROVERBS 20:24

God's Word reminds us of his power, his provision and his sovereignty.

*You are the God who performs miracles;
    you display your power among the peoples.
With your mighty arm you redeemed your people.*

PSALM 77:14–15

*Great is our Lord and mighty in power;
    his understanding has no limit.*

PSALM 147:5

*To God belong wisdom and power;
    counsel and understanding are his.*

JOB 12:13

*You are awesome, O God, in your sanctuary;
    the God of Israel gives power and strength to
        his people.*

PSALM 68:35

*The LORD saves his anointed;
    he answers him from his holy heaven
    with the saving power of his right hand.*

PSALM 20:6

Salvation and glory and power belong to our God.

REVELATION 19:1

His Word reminds us of his love.

We know and rely on the love God has for us.

How great is the love the Father has lavished on us, that we should be called children of God! And that is what we are!

As God's chosen people, holy and dearly loved, clothe yourselves with compassion, kindness, humility, gentleness and patience. Bear with each other and forgive whatever grievances you may have against one another. Forgive as the Lord forgave you. And over all these virtues put on love, which binds them all together in perfect unity

*I will never forget your precepts, Lord,
    for by them you have preserved my life.*

God has poured out his love into our hearts by the Holy Spirit, whom he has given us.

God demonstrates his own love for us in this: While we were still sinners, Christ died for us.

Greater love has no one than this, that he lay down his life for his friends.

Let's enjoy the time with God as he walks and talks with us each day, wherever we are.

I pray that out of his glorious riches he may strengthen you with power through his Spirit in your inner being, so that Christ may dwell in your hearts through faith. And I pray that you, being rooted and established in love, may have power, together with all the saints, to grasp how wide and long and high and deep is the love of Christ, and to know this love that surpasses knowledge—that you may be filled to the measure of all the fullness of God.

EPHESIANS 3:16–19

My mother taught me of God's love and promises from her knee. Every morning I would see her Bible and devotional book open on the kitchen table. She loved to pray, to attend church and prayer meetings. She taught her family the old hymns and choruses, and one favorite for me was (and still is):

Trust and obey for there is no other way,
to be happy in Jesus, is to trust and obey.
When we walk with the Lord in the light of his Word ...

Many times we neglect to thank God for his promises and his protection as he walks and talks with us each day, wherever we are, be it our own garden, or in the jungle, in the city or in the desert. Thank God for the daily guidance he provides. These prayers celebrate God's watchfulness and care.

GOD *Is* WITH US ...

DURING DIFFICULT TIMES
WHEN WE FEEL ALONE

*"But I'm aware that during the most
troublesome times of my life
there is only one set of footprints."*

Ruts and potholes. Shadows and deep darkness. The journey of life can sometimes be very troubling. We stumble and have difficulty following in God's footsteps. We are fearful of the unknown. But God's Word reminds us to trust, to believe, to hope.

When I am afraid,
  I will trust in you.
In God, whose word I praise,
  in God I trust; I will not be afraid.

PSALM 56:3–4

Have no fear of sudden disaster
  or of the ruin that overtakes the wicked,
for the LORD will be your confidence
  and will keep your foot from being snared.

PROVERBS 3:25–26

Everyone born of God overcomes the world. This is the victory that has overcome the world, even our faith. Who is it that overcomes the world? Only he who believes that Jesus is the Son of God.

1 JOHN 5:4–5

Let us then approach the throne of grace with confidence, so that we may receive mercy and find grace to help us in our time of need.

HEBREWS 4:16

The Lord delights in those who fear him,
  who put their hope in his unfailing love.

PSALM 147:11

Blessed is he whose help is the God of Jacob,
    whose hope is in the Lord his God,
the Maker of heaven and earth,
    the sea, and everything in them—
the Lord, who remains faithful forever.

PSALM 146:5–6

If you confess with your mouth, "Jesus is Lord," and believe in your heart that God raised him from the dead, you will be saved. For it is with your heart that you believe and are justified, and it is with your mouth that you confess and are saved.

ROMANS 10:9–10

Praise be to the God and Father of our Lord Jesus Christ! In his great mercy he has given us new birth into a living hope through the resurrection of Jesus Christ from the dead.

1 PETER 1:3

As for me, I watch in hope for the Lord,
    I wait for God my Savior;
    my God will hear me.

MICAH 7:7

This is the confidence we have in approaching God: that if we ask anything according to his will, he hears us. And if we know that he hears us—whatever we ask—we know that we have what we asked of him.

1 JOHN 5:14–15

We all go through troubling times, but we must never doubt God's presence with us.

God gives strength to the weary
and increases the power of the weak.

ISAIAH 40:29

You hear, O LORD, the desire of the afflicted;
you encourage them, and you listen to their cry.

PSALM 10:17

You are a shield around me, O LORD;
you bestow glory on me and lift up my head.
To the LORD I cry aloud,
and he answers me from his holy hill.

PSALM 3:3-4

God makes my feet like the feet of a deer;
he enables me to stand on the heights.
He trains my hands for battle;
my arms can bend a bow of bronze.
You give me your shield of victory,
and your right hand sustains me;
you stoop down to make me great.
You broaden the path beneath me,
so that my ankles do not turn.

PSALM 18:33-36

God will never let us down. He promises us his strength, his peace, his comfort and his presence. All we need to do is depend on him, for we can never break God's promises by leaning on them.

Do not be afraid. Stand firm and you will see the deliverance the LORD will bring you today. ...The LORD will fight for you; you need only to be still.

EXODUS 14:13–14

He who dwells in the shelter of the Most High
*   will rest in the shadow of the Almighty.*

PSALM 91:1

The LORD longs to be gracious to you;
*   he rises to show you compassion.*

ISAIAH 30:18

Evening, morning and noon
*   I cry out in distress,*
*   and God hears my voice.*

PSALM 55:17

The eyes of the LORD range throughout the earth to strengthen those whose hearts are fully committed to him.

2 CHRONICLES 16:9

I wait for you, O LORD;
  you will answer, O Lord my God.

PSALM 38:15

You will call, and the LORD will answer;
  you will cry for help, and he will say:
    Here am I.

ISAIAH 58:9

May you be richly rewarded by the LORD, the God of
Israel, under whose wings you have come to take refuge.

RUTH 2:12

I said to the LORD, "You are my Lord;
  apart from you I have no good thing."

PSALM 16:2

We know that in all things God works for the good of
those who love him, who have been called according to
his purpose.

ROMANS 8:28

God's divine power has given us everything we need
for life and godliness through our knowledge of him
who called us by his own glory and goodness.

2 PETER 1:3

I am still confident of this:
I will see the goodness of the LORD
in the land of the living.

PSALM 27:13

The LORD is good,
a refuge in times of trouble.
He cares for those who trust in him.

NAHUM 1:7

The LORD is good to all;
he has compassion on all he has made.

PSALM 145:9

God who began a good work in you will carry it on
to completion until the day of Christ Jesus.

PHILIPPIANS 1:6

God will keep you strong to the end, so that you will
be blameless on the day of our Lord Jesus Christ. God,
who has called you into fellowship with his Son Jesus
Christ our Lord, is faithful.

1 CORINTHIANS 1:8–9

Good and upright is the LORD;
therefore he instructs sinners in his ways.
He guides the humble in what is right
and teaches them his way.
All the ways of the LORD are loving and faithful
for those who keep the demands of his covenant.

PSALM 25:8–10

We must trust, believe, hope and continue to walk the path God has laid before us.

May our Lord Jesus Christ himself and God our Father, who loved us and by his grace gave us eternal encouragement and good hope, encourage your hearts and strengthen you in every good deed and word.

2 THESSALONIANS 2:16–17

There are times in life when we feel bereft, abandoned, alone. When loneliness overtakes us, we must remember that we are never alone. We can take comfort in God's promises to be with us—in our joy and in our pain, in the good times and in the bad times. God has promised that he will never forsake us. His steadfast love and faithfulness are promises we can cling to, promises that can bring us joy whenever we face the pangs of loneliness. Let us lean on these promises and receive God's peace. Let us walk in his footsteps and sense his strength. Let us stand in his presence and feel his love.

GOD *Is* WITH US ...

IN OUR CONFUSION

"*I just don't understand why, when I needed You most, You leave me.*"

I always prided myself on being able to find my way around any city or town throughout the world. Paul would just give me a map and I would head out, perhaps with one of my children as co-pilot in the passenger seat, and be certain of finding my destination with ease. I found that this sense of direction gave me great freedom and independence. When we moved to British Columbia, I seemed to have great difficulty in finding my way anywhere and I had to put my faith in Paul and the map to take us across rivers and over winding mountain roads. Often, it all conflicted with my sense of where north, south, east and west lay. I could not understand it; navigating had previously been so easy. Sometimes life can be much the same way; one minute you think you are on the right path and suddenly the path is filled with obstacles. When you become confused, remember you can ask God for directions.

This is what the Lord says—
"When you pass through the waters,
*   I will be with you;*
and when you pass through the rivers,
*   they will not sweep over you.*
When you walk through the fire,
*   you will not be burned;*
*   the flames will not set you ablaze."*

ISAIAH 43:1-2

When faced with bewildering circumstances we are tempted to ask "Why?" But a better question to ask is "What? … What do you have in mind now, Lord?"

The Spirit helps us in our weakness. We do not know what we ought to pray for, but the Spirit himself intercedes for us with groans that words cannot express. And he who searches our hearts knows the mind of the Spirit, because the Spirit intercedes for the saints in accordance with God's will.

ROMANS 8:26–27

O LORD, I call to you; come quickly to me.
 Hear my voice when I call to you.
May my prayer be set before you like incense;
 may the lifting up of my hands be like the
  evening sacrifice.

PSALM 141:1–2

I call on the LORD in my distress,
 and he answers me.

PSALM 120:1

I love the LORD, for he heard my voice;
 he heard my cry for mercy.
Because he turned his ear to me,
 I will call on him as long as I live.

PSALM 116:1–2

Though it may sometimes seem that things are out of control, we can take comfort in God's enduring promises and constant presence.

"You will seek me and find me when you seek me with all your heart. I will be found by you," declares the LORD.

JEREMIAH 29:13–14

Jesus said, "My sheep listen to my voice; I know them, and they follow me. I give them eternal life, and they shall never perish; no one can snatch them out of my hand. My Father, who has given them to me, is greater than all; no one can snatch them out of my Father's hand. I and the Father are one."

JOHN 10:27–30

"I the LORD do not change," says the LORD Almighty.

MALACHI 3:6

*The LORD is good and his love endures forever;
his faithfulness continues through all generations.*

PSALM 100:5

God, who has called you into fellowship with his Son Jesus Christ our Lord, is faithful.

1 CORINTHIANS 1:9

You, O Lord, are a compassionate and gracious God,
  slow to anger, abounding in love and faithfulness.

PSALM 86:15

Who is a God like you,
  who pardons sin and forgives the transgression
  of the remnant of his inheritance?
You do not stay angry forever
  but delight to show mercy.
You will again have compassion on us.

MICAH 7:18—19

God's mercy extends to those who fear him,
  from generation to generation.

LUKE 1:50

Our citizenship is in heaven. And we eagerly await a
Savior from there, the Lord Jesus Christ, who, by the
power that enables him to bring everything under his
control, will transform our lowly bodies so that they
will be like his glorious body.

PHILIPPIANS 3:20—21

"I am bringing my righteousness near,
  it is not far away;
  and my salvation will not be delayed,"
    says the Lord.

ISAIAH 46:13

Blessed are you who hunger now,
for you will be satisfied.
Blessed are you who weep now,
for you will laugh.

LUKE 6:21

Put away all doubts. Cast out all confusion. Stand firm in the work of the Lord and find a renewed faith following in his footsteps.

Arise, shine, for your light has come,
and the glory of the LORD rises upon you.
See, darkness covers the earth
and thick darkness is over the peoples,
but the LORD rises upon you
and his glory appears over you.

ISAIAH 60:1–2

God always has a plan. God always has a purpose in every situation for those who follow in his footsteps. When we experience God's forgiveness, we are new creatures. God's presence is with us to help us, even when we don't realize it. There is hope. There is a light in the darkness. Jesus Christ, God's Son, can strengthen our faith if we will wait patiently and trust in God's desire to make us more like himself. We must put away all doubts. Cast out all confusion. Then we will find a renewed faith as we follow in his footsteps.

GOD *Is* WITH US ...

AS OUR LOVING FATHER

He whispered,
"My precious child ..."

he Creator of the universe calls us his children—what a blessing! What a privilege! What a responsibility!

The LORD disciplines those he loves,
   as a father the son he delights in.

              PROVERBS 3:12

"I will be a Father to you,
   and you will be my sons and daughters,"
     says the Lord Almighty.

         2 CORINTHIANS 6:18

To all who received him, to those who believed in his name, he gave the right to become children of God—children born not of natural descent, nor of human decision or a husband's will, but born of God.

           JOHN 1:12–13

You are my Father,
   my God, the Rock my Savior.

            PSALM 89:26

To us a child is born,
   to us a son is given. . . .
And he will be called . . .
   Everlasting Father.

            ISAIAH 9:6

O LORD, you are our Father.
   We are the clay, you are the potter;
   we are all the work of your hand.

            ISAIAH 64:8

The Spirit himself testifies with our spirit that we are God's children. Now if we are children, then we are heirs—heirs of God and co-heirs with Christ, if indeed we share in his sufferings in order that we may also share in his glory.

ROMANS 8:16–17

For us there is but one God, the Father, from whom all things came and for whom we live; and there is but one Lord, Jesus Christ, through whom all things came and through whom we live.

1 CORINTHIANS 8:6

There is one body and one Spirit—just as you were called to one hope when you were called—one Lord, one faith, one baptism; one God and Father of all, who is over all and through all and in all.

EPHESIANS 4:4–6

Those who are led by the Spirit of God are sons of God. For you did not receive a spirit that makes you a slave again to fear, but you received the Spirit of sonship. And by him we cry, "Abba, Father."

ROMANS 8:14–15

As children of God we can trust that our Father will provide for us.

Jesus said, "Your Father knows what you need before you ask him."

MATTHEW 6:8

Jesus said, "Which of you fathers, if your son asks for a fish, will give him a snake instead? Or if he asks for an egg, will give him a scorpion? If you then, though you are evil, know how to give good gifts to your children, how much more will your Father in heaven give the Holy Spirit to those who ask him!"

LUKE 11:11–13

God will meet all your needs according to his glorious riches in Christ Jesus.

PHILIPPIANS 4:19

God is able to make all grace abound to you, so that in all things at all times, having all that you need, you will abound in every good work.

2 CORINTHIANS 9:8

As God's children, our Father knows us by name and bestows on us certain rights, privileges and responsibilities.

Praise be to the God and Father of our Lord Jesus Christ, who has blessed us in the heavenly realms with every spiritual blessing in Christ. For he chose us in him before the creation of the world to be holy and blameless in his sight. In love he predestined us to be adopted as his sons through Jesus Christ, in accordance with his pleasure and will—to the praise of his glorious grace, which he has freely given us in the One he loves.

EPHESIANS 1:3–6

Before I was born the LORD called me;
  from my birth he has made mention of my name.

ISAIAH 49:1

It was because the LORD loved you and kept the oath he swore to your forefathers that he brought you out with a mighty hand and redeemed you.

DEUTERONOMY 7:8

When the kindness and love of God our Savior appeared, he saved us, not because of righteous things we had done, but because of his mercy. He saved us through the washing of rebirth and renewal by the Holy Spirit, whom he poured out on us generously through Jesus Christ our Savior, so that, having been justified by his grace, we might become heirs having the hope of eternal life.

TITUS 3:4–7

Praise be to the God and Father of our Lord Jesus Christ! In his great mercy he has given us new birth into a living hope through the resurrection of Jesus Christ from the dead, and into an inheritance that can never perish, spoil or fade—kept in heaven for you, who through faith are shielded by God's power until the coming of the salvation that is ready to be revealed in the last time.

1 PETER 1:3–5

Our loving Father cares for us as a shepherd cares for his sheep. And we, his children, need to listen carefully to his voice.

Jesus said, "The sheep listen to [the shepherd's] voice. He calls his own sheep by name and leads them out. When he has brought out all his own, he goes on ahead of them, and his sheep follow him because they know his voice."

JOHN 10:3–4

Jesus said, "I am the good shepherd; I know my sheep and my sheep know me—just as the Father knows me and I know the Father—and I lay down my life for the sheep."

JOHN 10:14–15

Know that the LORD is God.
It is he who made us, and we are his;
we are his people, the sheep of his pasture.

PSALM 100:3

The Lord tends his flock like a shepherd:
He gathers the lambs in his arms
and carries them close to his heart;
he gently leads those that have young.

ISAIAH 40:11

I remember my father having a kind of intimate, heartfelt compassion with me. Often when my dad would be busy at his easel, I'd sit on the floor at his side with my crayons and coloring book. Sometimes he'd set his brushes aside, reach down and lift me into his lap. Then he'd fix my hand on one of his brushes and enfold his larger, stronger hand around mine. Ever so gently, he would guide my hand and the brush, and I would watch in amazement as, together, we made something beautiful. This is the kind of love our God has for us. Fatherlove. The kind, gentle compassion of a dad who deeply cares for his sons and daughters. … Let God's big hand close gently over yours. With his help, even the discouraging scribbles of your life can become a masterpiece. Nothing would delight a father's heart more.

Joni Eareckson Tada

GOD *Is* WITH US ...

ALWAYS!

"I love you and will never leave you never, ever, during your trials and testings."

We *often make promises* we can't keep. God isn't like that. God is faithful and trustworthy. When God promises never to leave us, he means just what he says. He's not going anywhere!

"Even to your old age and gray hairs
I am he, I am he who will sustain you.
I have made you and I will carry you;
I will sustain you and I will rescue you,"
says the LORD.

ISAIAH 46:4

I was young and now I am old,
yet I have never seen the righteous forsaken
or their children begging bread.
They are always generous and lend freely;
their children will be blessed.

PSALM 37:25–26

May your whole spirit, soul and body be kept blameless at the coming of our Lord Jesus Christ. The one who calls you is faithful and he will do it.

1 THESSALONIANS 5:23–24

Do not forget this one thing, dear friends: With the Lord a day is like a thousand years, and a thousand years are like a day. The Lord is not slow in keeping his promise, as some understand slowness. He is patient with you.

2 PETER 3:8–9

The works of God's hands are faithful and just;
    all his precepts are trustworthy.
They are steadfast for ever and ever,
    done in faithfulness and uprightness.

PSALM 111:7−8

If we confess our sins, God is faithful and just and will forgive us our sins and purify us from all unrighteousness.

1 JOHN 1:9

The Lord is faithful, and he will strengthen and protect you from the evil one.

2 THESSALONIANS 3:3

The LORD is faithful to all his promises
    and loving toward all he has made.

PSALM 145:13

Since we have been justified through faith, we have peace with God through our Lord Jesus Christ, through whom we have gained access by faith into this grace in which we now stand. And we rejoice in the hope of the glory of God.

ROMANS 5:1−2

No matter how many promises God has made, they are "Yes" in Christ. And so through him the "Amen" is spoken by us to the glory of God. Now it is God who makes both us and you stand firm in Christ. He anointed us, set his seal of ownership on us, and put his Spirit in our hearts as a deposit, guaranteeing what is to come.

2 CORINTHIANS 1:20–22

God has shown kindness by giving you rain from heaven and crops in their seasons; he provides you with plenty of food and fills your hearts with joy.

ACTS 14:17

Jesus said, "See how the lilies of the field grow. They do not labor or spin. Yet I tell you that not even Solomon in all his splendor was dressed like one of these. If that is how God clothes the grass of the field, which is here today and tomorrow is thrown into the fire, will he not much more clothe you, O you of little faith? So do not worry, saying, 'What shall we eat?' or 'What shall we drink?' or 'What shall we wear?' . . . Your heavenly Father knows that you need them. But seek first his kingdom and his righteousness, and all these things will be given to you as well."

MATTHEW 6:28–33

When it seems that life is whirling out of control, we can take comfort in God's sovereignty and power. He has everything under control. And he will work his will in every circumstance.

Many are the plans in a man's heart,
    but it is the LORD'S purpose that prevails.

PROVERBS 19:21

I know that you can do all things;
    no plan of yours can be thwarted, LORD.

JOB 42:2

Gideon told them, "I will not rule over you, nor will my son rule over you. The LORD will rule over you."

JUDGES 8:23

God's abundant provision of grace and of the gift of righteousness reign in life through the one man, Jesus Christ.

ROMANS 5:17

"What I have said, that will I bring about;
    what I have planned, that will I do," says the Lord.

ISAIAH 46:11

"I am God, and there is no other;
   I am God, and there is none like me.
I make known the end from the beginning,
   from ancient times, what is still to come.
I say: My purpose will stand,
   and I will do all that I please."

ISAIAH 46:9–10

The earth is the LORD's, and everything in it,
   the world, and all who live in it.

PSALM 24:1

The LORD Almighty has purposed, and who can
   thwart him?
   His hand is stretched out, and who can turn
      it back?

ISAIAH 14:27

I cry out to God Most High,
   to God, who fulfills his purpose for me.

PSALM 57:2

I have labored to no purpose;
   I have spent my strength in vain and for nothing.
Yet what is due me is in the LORD's hand,
   and my reward is with my God.

ISAIAH 49:4

I will come and proclaim your mighty acts,
    O Sovereign LORD;
    I will proclaim your righteousness, yours alone.
Since my youth, O God, you have taught me,
    and to this day I declare your marvelous deeds.
Even when I am old and gray,
    do not forsake me, O God,
till I declare your power to the next generation,
    your might to all who are to come.

PSALM 71:16–18

Whenever we hit rock-bottom, we can be assured
of God's love and care. His encouragement breathes
new possibilities into impossible circumstances.

In you, O LORD, I have taken refuge;
    let me never be put to shame;
    deliver me in your righteousness.

PSALM 31:1

Those who trust in the LORD are like Mount Zion,
    which cannot be shaken but endures forever.

PSALM 125:1

The LORD is with me; I will not be afraid.

PSALM 118:6

Taste and see that the LORD is good;
    blessed is the man who takes refuge in him.

PSALM 34:8

The eyes of the LORD are on those who fear him,
    on those whose hope is in his unfailing love.

PSALM 33:18

Though we may face trouble and difficulties, sadness and pain, God is still in control, and he is always with us. When trouble rages, we must listen closely to God's voice. When the agonies of life begin to bear down upon us, God has not moved away from us. We may have moved away from him. We must return to him in faith and call on him for his strength. He wants to bring us his divine comfort. Though things may seem hopeless, no trial is so great that God cannot deliver us, no pain is so great that he cannot bring us comfort, no circumstance is ever without God's presence. When God promises never to leave us, he means just that. He is in control.

GOD *Is* WITH US ...

AS OUR STRONG PROVIDER

*"When you saw only one set of
footprints
it was then that I carried you."*

*I*t was around midnight when we finished our prayer time, and we had been praying for our married daughter and son-in-law who had left earlier that day after a short stay with us. We were expecting to hear from them about eight o'clock. ... Paul decided he couldn't wait any longer. Just as he picked up the phone to dial their number he heard their voices at the other end! There had been no telephone ring at our end of the line. They had just arrived and were about to telephone us, but the call connected without anyone dialing. They related a testimony of God's saving presence. On the way, they had missed their regular turn-off for gas and refreshments. ... They had taken the next exit off the freeway, and had doubled back into a town called Hope. They found a gas station open, and stopped to get a fill-up. ... When paying their bill, they heard on the emergency radio in the station a highway patrol announcement of a major snow and earth slide across the highway at the very place they would have been had they made their normal stop. An extra detour meant they arrived home tired and weary, but in one piece.

"I am the Lord, the God of all mankind. Is anything too hard for me?"

JEREMIAH 32:27

With God all things are possible.

MATTHEW 19:26

*In the LORD alone
    are righteousness and strength.*

ISAIAH 45:24

*They cried out to the LORD in their trouble,
    and he delivered them from their distress.*

PSALM 107:6

*Do you not know?
    Have you not heard?
The LORD is the everlasting God,
    the Creator of the ends of the earth.
He will not grow tired or weary,
    and his understanding no one can fathom.*

ISAIAH 40:28

*The LORD is the strength of his people,
    a fortress of salvation for his anointed one.*

PSALM 28:8

*The arm of the LORD is not too short to save,
    nor his ear too dull to hear.*

ISAIAH 59:1

The Lord will rescue me from every evil attack and will bring me safely to his heavenly kingdom. To him be glory for ever and ever.

2 TIMOTHY 4:18

Your light will break forth like the dawn,
    and your healing will quickly appear;
then your righteousness will go before you,
    and the glory of the LORD will be your rear
        guard.

ISAIAH 58:8

Since God is our strong provider, we can be assured that he is in control of every aspect of our lives. He will prepare the way before us. He will never leave us. And he will provide our every need.

He lifted me out of the slimy pit,
    out of the mud and mire;
he set my feet on a rock
    and gave me a firm place to stand.
He put a new song in my mouth,
    a hymn of praise to our God.
Many will see and fear
    and put their trust in the LORD.

PSALM 40:2–3

Be glad, O people of Zion,
   rejoice in the LORD your God,
for he has given you
   the autumn rains in righteousness.
He sends you abundant showers,
   both autumn and spring rains, as before.

JOEL 2:23

Command those who are rich in this present world ...
to put their hope in God, who richly provides us with
everything for our enjoyment.

1 TIMOTHY 6:17

He who did not spare his own Son, but gave him up
for us all—how will he not also, along with him, gra-
ciously give us all things?

ROMANS 8:32

Praise the LORD, O my soul,
and forget not all his benefits—
   who forgives all your sins
and heals all your diseases,
   who redeems your life from the pit
and crowns you with love and compassion,
   who satisfies your desires with good things
so that your youth is renewed like the eagle's.

PSALM 103:2—5

Our God is strong enough to carry us, but also gentle enough to enfold us in his loving embrace.

The Sovereign LORD says: I myself will search for my sheep and look after them. As a shepherd looks after his scattered flock when he is with them, so will I look after my sheep. I will rescue them from all the places where they were scattered on a day of clouds and darkness.

EZEKIEL 34:11–12

*God will command his angels concerning you
    to guard you carefully;
they will lift you up in their hands,
    so that you will not strike your foot against a stone.*

PSALM 91:11–12

*As a father has compassion on his children,
    so the LORD has compassion on those
        who fear him;
for he knows how we are formed,
    he remembers that we are dust.*

PSALM 103:13–14

*I will betroth you to me forever;
    I will betroth you in righteousness and justice,
    in love and compassion.
I will betroth you in faithfulness,
    and you will acknowledge the LORD.*

HOSEA 2:19–20

As our strong provider carries us over the rough places in our lives, he speaks words of peace and blessing to our wounded hearts.

The LORD bless you
and keep you;
the LORD make his face shine upon you
and be gracious to you;
the LORD turn his face toward you
and give you peace.

NUMBERS 6:24–26

May the God of peace, who through the blood of the eternal covenant brought back from the dead our Lord Jesus, that great Shepherd of the sheep, equip you with everything good for doing his will, and may he work in us what is pleasing to him, through Jesus Christ, to whom be glory for ever and ever. Amen.

HEBREWS 13:20–21

Though it seems as if the whole world has gone wrong around us, we are not alone. God is with us! He will prepare the way before us. ... All we need to do is trust in God's loving companionship as we walk closely with him, and he will bring blessing into our lives. Our heavenly Father is faithful and will never leave us or forsake us. As we come to him daily, willing to be directed, he will guide us with his word, shape us by our experiences, and stamp his signature on our lives as we follow in his footsteps.

At Inspirio we love to hear from you—
your stories, your feedback,
and your product ideas.
Please send your comments to us
by way of e-mail at
icares@zondervan.com
or to the address below:

Attn: Inspirio Cares
5300 Patterson Avenue SE
Grand Rapids, MI 49530

If you would like further information
about Inspirio and the products we
create please visit us at:
www.inspiriogifts.com

Thank you and God Bless!